MAD RIVER

1994 Agnes Lynch Starrett Poetry Prize

MAD RIVER

JAN BEATTY

University of Pittsburgh Press

The publication of this book is supported by a grant from the Pennsylvania Council on the Arts.

Published by the University of Pittsburgh Press, Pittsburgh, Pa. 15260
Copyright © 1995, Jan Beatty
All rights reserved
Manufactured in the United States of America
Printed on acid-free paper
10 9 8 7 6 5 4 3 2

Library of Congress Cataloging-in-Publication Data

Beatty, Jan.
Mad river / Jan Beatty
      p.   cm. — (Pitt poetry series)
   ISBN 0-8229-3897-9 (cl.).—ISBN 0-8229-5570-9 (pbk.)
    I. Title.   II. Series.
PS3552.E179M3   1995   95-31468
811'.54—dc20   CIP

A CIP catalog record for this book is available from the British Library.
Eurospan, London

Paperback cover and title page art: "Mad River" by Michel Tsouris. Courtesy of Elizabeth Bennett and Paul Colaiaco.

Book Design: Frank Lehner

for Robert T. Beatty

CONTENTS

I

If This Is Sex, It Must Be Tuesday 5

Mad River 6

Grabbing at Beauty 7

What We Can Count On 8

The Rolling Rock Man 9

Pittsburgh Poem 11

The Order of Things 12

1,200 lb. Man Starts on Road to 190 lbs. 14

Fifteen Minutes at the Dairy Mart 15

Ravenous Blue 16

Leonard Avenue 17

II

Highway 99 21

Getting Through 23

Letter to Mario 25

As If That's All There Is 26

Awake in a Strange Landscape 27

An Abortion Attempt by my Mother 29

Morning Radio 30

fifteen 31

Ferry at Night 32

Watching My Father 33

Fog 34

Dream with No Words 35

Sucking 36

Self-Hatred 37

Walking in Shade 38

Wanting to Continue 39

III

Saving the Crippled Boy   43

What I Want   45

Introducing You to My Dead Father   46

Breaking the Skin   47

after sex on a train   48

Love Poem   49

Visiting My Father a Few Days Before His Operation   50

Ghost Orchid   52

The Space That Remains   53

A Waitress' Instructions on Tipping or
    Get the Cash Up and Don't Waste My Time   54

T-shirts   55

Standing by the McKenzie River at Night   56

Blue Dress   57

Not Thinking About Gardenias   58

Asking the Dead for Help   59

The Flower Garden   60

One Hand on the Door   61

Free World   62

Acknowledgments   63

MAD RIVER

I

Not lost, but abandoned,
Left behind;
This is my hand
Upon your mind.
   —LOUISE BOGAN

IF THIS IS SEX, IT MUST BE TUESDAY

So it was every week on a Tuesday,
that you and your friend, Ginny,
strayed from the dance at St. Anselm's
to Duquesne Gardens, feigning interest
in hockey, waiting to get laid.
I can picture it—you in fake cashmere
with pearl buttons, a gabardine skirt
that hit you at midcalf, you and Ginny
shuffling popcorn till last period,
when you'd freshen your lips with TORRID RED
for the after game party at the Webster Hall dorms.
After all, these were the Pittsburgh Hornets,
this was 1951, and you were a poor Irish girl
from Garfield with a hard drive for excitement,
and hockey was it, getting cross-checked by the best,
having stories to tell in your lean, checkered life,
left with no father, a reluctant sister,
and a mother who cleaned houses for the rich.
So when did I happen, this one-night stand
with the MVP after his big, icy win,
the second Tuesday in February, or the third?
Do you remember the feel of his hands on you?
Were they rough, or tender, were they bloody
from fighting? And when your belly grew into
the body you never wanted, did you curse me,
try to cut me? Should I say you did your best,
a spare girl from a broken family,
or should I say it straight—
you wanted it, you took it, like we all do,
you lied to save yourself, you gave away
part of your heart, you couldn't
wish it right.

MAD RIVER

Two dollars and sixty-five cents
at the Hot Spot Take-Out Shack
for one chili dog and a coke,
Birmingham, Alabama, 1979.
I kissed a Greyhound bus driver
too many times so I could eat,
I got one chili dog, I wanted two,
thought I'd get two. Lucky I'm not dead.
I asked him about his children, his
fourteen-year-old daughter saved my life,
pulled up his rotten conscience like
regurgitation, black bile memory—I said
How old is your daughter, afraid he'd want
more for his money, and in the slant light
of his dark Chevy he saw a slice
of my young girl face and said,
She's fourteen, I better get you back
to the depot, and the black stench
of his twisted conscience wanted one more
kiss, one more kiss to get me back
to the bus station and my long ride home,
to wanting to spit up the dark beans,
their reddish bodies staining my insides
like a dead baby, like a blood spill,
my heart pumping its mad river with
sixty cents in my pocket and twenty-six
hours till home, I prayed for rain,
I prayed for morning.

GRABBING AT BEAUTY

The retarded man in the post office
asked for the stamps with pictures of the sea on them—
he didn't say ocean, or water;
His head stayed cocked to the side as he talked,
as he stared beyond the heads of people.
I didn't know that later that night,
I would stare at the moon with my head tilted,
trying to see a trace of what he sees,
knowing that I couldn't.
The moon held its expected place in the sky,
the sidewalks cracked no differently that night—
I called my friend Kathy and took her out
for a birthday dinner three months late,
told her I missed her as I gulped
the champagne, wanting to speed everything up.
Outside, the streets carried on as if
the normal were occurring, as if we weren't
rushing at each other, grabbing at beauty,
as if the sea never existed at all.
We went to Frankie's bar, where the band
played "Johnny B. Goode" slow and even,
just like it should never be played.

WHAT WE CAN COUNT ON

Squeezing between the two trees, I look for beads of water
on the leaves of the azalea, knowing the six inches between them
will let me through. I count on feeling wild azalea
on my stomach and back. It's not at all like being touched
by a man, roaming fingers and hands, someone who
can't breathe another moment without pressing against me.
I want something pushing back, to be surrounded by more than air.

I think of two little girls I knew once, and how they were kept
in a closet by their parents. What pushed against *them?*
I know they weren't fed. Was it their father's cotton shirt,
the smell of cedar and feces, the pale skin of their faces
against each other?

I was their social worker. I took them to the park—I thought
Openness—I let them choose what food to eat, they chose to wait
in the car, they wanted me to decide, I bought take-out pizza
and found them leaning against each other in the front seat,
playing with the beige upholstery of my old Pontiac, touching
the knobs for heat and cold, sticking their small faces
toward the stale air.

THE ROLLING ROCK MAN

It's not me shouting at no one
in Cadillac Square: it's God
roaring inside me, afraid
to be alone.

—LAWRENCE JOSEPH

Never talks, never tips,
drinks two Rolling Rock draughts,
maybe three as he sits for hours
in the restaurant, wears too many clothes
for the weather, his combat jacket,
his navy blue cap, oblivious
to the people eating lunch around him.
Can I get you something to drink? I say,
afraid to say, *How about a Rolling Rock,*
afraid to be familiar with a man like this.
Somebody already waited on me, he said.
Okay, good, I said.
You lost some weight.
Yeah, I said, *a little,*
amazed that he is speaking, that
he has noticed a change in me.
I look straight at him, one of his eyes
is blood, a red blotch from a punch—
he said, *You look like you have AIDS,*
you better go to the hospital,
you're gonna die soon.
I felt the evil wash over me
as I walked to my next table, stunned
by this backwash of words, this bold

sickness, this butcher world that's in
and around us, *Someone please, pray for us.*
Minutes later, he started shouting at no one,
Body bags, he yelled, *Body bags.*
I heard the words as I watched a five-year-old girl
stare at him, afraid for her. *Vietnam,* he shouted,
as customers looked up from their chicken salads,
women three feet away sucked Bloody Marys
and fingered their circle pins—he heard a song
and he spoke the words—I don't know
what he saw or heard.

PITTSBURGH POEM

On Sarah Street on the South Side,
the old woman still stands with her broom, imagining
the air full of lug and swish from the steelworker's boot,
armies of gray lunchbuckets grace her thoughts
as she sweeps with the part of her that still believes;
sweeps while her sister makes paska and horseradish with red beets,
sweeps away the stains of a dead husband and a disappointing daughter.

She thinks of the dark well of J & L, how it sifted down to nothing,
the mill's hole of a mouth that ate full years of her life,
nights she pulled her husband from Yarsky's bar across the street,
him smiling like a bagful of dimes, half a paycheck spent,
the whole time soot covering their clothes, the car, the windowsills,
like disease, someone else's hands.

She holds tight onto the good times, the new green velour couch,
Saturday walks to the Markethouse for fresh red cabbage and greens,
trips to the Brown & Green store for new T-shirts, South Side windows
brimming taffeta and satin on the way to Mass at St. Michael's,
when the world was gleaming and available for one glorious day.

Now shadows angle across her print housedress and she holds tight
to her broom, hears her sister primping in the kitchen, smells the pea soup
with sauerkraut, the homemade mushroom gravy for perogies, she thinks
of the ten years since her husband died, of her daughter who calls
on holidays, she stands on her concrete lawn,
taking care of something invisible, the listless air,
her life.

The Order of Things

So it's late September and my phone's been shut off,
I'm walking through Oakland, brimming with bad credit,
imagining lunch, when I see a blind man snapping
his white cane at the utility pole on the corner of Forbes
and Atwood, his face aimed straight at the sky.

He's demanding to know the order of things,
as he taps the glass of the Rite-Aid door, skims
the metal of the *New York Times* machine. I watch
sneakily, ashamed, knowing he'll find his way today
by slapping the world with a stick, knowing I'm afraid
of the dark, still sleep with a light on, not knowing
if it's blackness he sees, or some faint, retrograde shadow.

Excuse me, he says to the air, *Can you tell me
when the WALK sign comes on?* Sighted people spin
around, making nervous eye contact with each other—who
is he talking to? *Sure*, I say, wondering just
what's in his briefcase, who picked out his suit—
it's ugly and brown, would he wear it if he knew?

And had he ever seen his huge teeth, his pasty skin?
I turn to face the side of his face, and say,
*Don't they have beepers in some cities to let you know
when to walk?* My eagerness oozed like an illness,
he swung toward me, eyes all white light and fury,
said, *We fought for three years to have that system
at Fifth and Craig—it's called the wheels of justice.*

Something churning inside me had to know—who combs
his hair, is he happy? *The WALK sign, it's on,* I said,
They're slow, he said, *if they move at all.*
He thrashed his head back, laughed too loud with
his mouthful of teeth—bodies scattered before him
as he swung his cane wide—right to left, and left
me at the corner with my own urgent self.

1,200 LB. MAN STARTS ON ROAD TO 190 LBS.

—in memory of Walter Hudson

Who braided Walter Hudson's hair?
It lies, two thin strings
across the ocean of his flesh. His hair,
wrapped with tight care by... his mother?
Walter cannot lift his arms to his head.
The paper said that Walter "spends
his days lying under a sheet in bed
and is cared for by his family."

Is it his sister?
Does she kneel by his head and tend to his hair
as he lies under sheets and fills, fills?
Is there a friend who comes
and strokes his head and sees
the man inside the prison of his skin?

On the ten foot journey to the bathroom,
Walter lifts rolls of himself forward,
shifting flesh for forty minutes,
panting and wheezing, he dreams
of what? The paper quotes him:
"I want to do something with my life
before I pass on to the next world."

FIFTEEN MINUTES AT THE DAIRY MART

Do you want to party with a male stripper?
I look in the window of the black Buick and say, *No.*
What's the matter, don't you party?
No, no, I don't party, I lie. I cross the street,
immediately change my mind, and look for him.
No sign. I walk into the Dairy Mart and wait for a ride.
A tiny woman comes in and begins to talk to the bread.
I want a small loaf of bread. The woman behind the counter
says that she has left her hearing aid at home.
She keeps saying, *What's that, honey?* to everyone.
The tiny woman is looking for ham, now, no salt.
I am thinking of the boy in the black Buick, his dark eyes and black hair.
A man with two coats on pulls a shivering terrier into the store
and offers me a ride. *I just saw you standing there
and thought I could help,* he said. *I'm fine,* I said.
You can't have that dog in here! the counter woman yells.
Now the tiny woman wants a plain danish, round, not square, no walnuts.
What's that, honey? A business type in a topcoat buys a pack of gum.
Do you have anything in your pockets? the counter woman says.
He shakes his head and leaves the store. *Every time he's here
he steals something,* she says. *I saw him, I saw him
put something in his pocket.* The tiny woman leaves with nothing.
I drink chocolate milk and think about saying yes.

Ravenous Blue

—*in memory of Scott Prather*

We drive up to visit you, talking about school and work,
we don't say you've gone blind, we don't talk about AIDS.
In your mother's living room, you sit on a chair
with blue foam padding, your body too thin to bear
its own weight. I keep looking at the blue,
ravenous blue, remember? We were stoned and running
up and down the aisles of the beauty supply store,
looking for hair color, when I saw RAVENOUS BLUE,
and fell in love with the name.
You tried to talk me out of it, but we dyed
my hair from blond to blue, and shortly after,
young boys in leather started trying to pick me up,
mistaking me for a young thrasher.
The color was so dark, we couldn't cover it,
so we just laughed until it grew out, but
now we're here, just us and this pressing air,
your wide, blind stare, the words we don't say,
and I'm so sorry we are here,
and this is you,
dying.

LEONARD AVENUE

Walking down Leonard Avenue
thinking of cheap wine
and missionary sex I pass
an old woman and remember
the smell of army blankets
in the woods, not wanting
to wash the mud off,
spiders tickling my neck
you walking away to piss
me drowning in extended orgasm
your arm around my back
the key to every universe, your tongue
the messenger of a life around the corner,
where are you now?
I'd walk a mile to feel
your hand between my legs
to smell your neck—my God—
is there anyone I can say this to—
the men are hissing and slapping
outside of BJ's bar, cars move past
hot glitter in the sun
I'm looking for a boy with a scarred face,
something to tell me he'll explode, not run
in a storm. He'll let loose all the words
I've kept stuffed in these old stories—
he'll rage like a brown river flooding,
he'll say, *Easy*
he'll say, *Let go.*
We'll find open water.

II

When your soul is heavy
it turns to water.
—EDIE RENO

Highway 99

Riding down Highway 99 on the back
of a cobalt blue Harley, no helmet,
with some guy named Wild Bill, my red
bandanna snapping in the hot night air,
a six pack of Pabst in the saddlebags,
I knew I had found the slick heart
of freedom, California style, on those
midnight roads from San Francisco to Fresno,
we were in-transit, strapped in by the wind,
and I wished my life on everyone breathing.

Just one hour into morning, my high fading
like a wicked joke, I slapped his back,
he yelled, *We're almost there.*
Five minutes into his faded pink trailer
on this cheap fifties mohair couch,
he pulls out a mugshot of himself, numbers and all.
Even through the beer haze, I knew I was stupid,
my wild self collapsing flat inside me, my heart
speeding into fear, as I said, *What were you
in for?* and he said, *Rape*, with a sick,
greasy smile like backwash, like a cold black
wave that made me look at the trees outside,
and I felt something hard rise inside me, like
another person, another me, and I asked him
if he'd ever want to hurt me—he hung his head
like a drowned man, said, *No, I guess not,*
and I said to his barrel chest, his huge arms,
that I wanted to go home, and then god picked up
my heart and we rode back, the sissy bar holding me,

and I couldn't think of one friend I had in life.
The bay looked like the only safe place,
dark and thick with the words of the ones
who never lived to say this—I am telling you
so you'll know—that the black glue of the night,
the half-mast moon over a double line, the
cobalt blue couldn't bring me back.

Getting Through

You're gonna have to take those boots off, he said,
guarding the metal detector with a steady smirk,
Okay, I said, wondering if I'd worn my good socks.
Already I had stopped at the water fountain, loitered
by the lockers, gone to the bathroom to delay this exchange.
Those earrings gotta go, too, he said,
Yeah, I said, knowing that he liked to pick fights.
You the teacher? Yes, I said, and
he started to chuckle, said, *What do you teach?*
Creative writing, I said, and he let out a loud snort,
You think these guys give a shit about creative writing?
They're usin' this to look good for parole,
so they can get out and kill somebody else—
Now do you like helpin' them do that?

He hooked me with this one, like he did every week,
I stared into his twisted face, half smile/half hate,
the machine was beeping wildly, I knew I should just shrug,
I needed him to get in, had to see him every week.
Got any change on ya? Sometimes that'll set it off.
This was the thing that scared me most about him—
sometimes he sounded so kind—that split between sweet
and vicious, someone you wouldn't want to have breakfast with.
I wanted to disappear into the wall, into the line
of anxious visitors behind me, so they couldn't see,
so they couldn't hear him harass me.

So you think these guys deserve to be taught?
Yes, I do, I said clearly, watching him treat me
like some naïve cartoon, *I've seen so many*
young teachers like you, you don't know anything.

Should I scream at him, should I go in and teach,
Okay, I said, *See ya later,* I said,
as if it didn't bother me, as if it didn't
set off a slow burning inside me—
he pushed the button, the metal doors slid open,
I headed toward the unruly yard, head down.

LETTER TO MARIO

Your hand goes up, your tone as earnest as an armed robbery.
I don't know your past, if you've killed or raped, you speak a
broken English, eyes alert as a found victim, this is maximum
security, this is you sitting in the back with your stack of books,
and me feeling my way through a dark hallway, and you are old,
with a steel wool mustache, spouting fractured words, jumble
of sounds, I strain to listen like a woman afraid
of intruders, ask you to repeat, and you do, again and
again and I look to the other inmates for help, and they shrug,
don't want to get involved, and say—*Nobody ever understands
him*—they have their own concerns, their short story
with a sick twist, their wounded poems, so I try to take
just one of your words and stretch it with a guess, expand
from the air, you shake your head and I know I haven't heard you
again—I can't cross this ground—I'm leaving you.
I am the next, the one more, another who hasn't heard you,
I move on because the rest of the class is bored, and
I don't know what else to try, and what else is there
to say—that your trust was sniped and gutted as a child,
that the prison wants you to rot, that I'm drowning in my own
thick limits, and all I can feel are your earnest eyes, and
this is not good enough, not even close, and here it is again,
us and them, and I can see why you'd hate, in this brick, cold
house in another country, and no syllables we say, no longing
for gods and revolutions can set it right.

As If That's All There Is

Don't ask me to ponder the shape
of an old oak bench, or why
in the sixteenth century things were
as they were, as if that's all there is.

I'm not so impressed with your studies
as I watch you talk to a guy in a bar
and miss the essence of the conversation.

You are an oak table, your careful words
a testament to someone's craftsmanship.
You hear only what you're about to say next.

I know you'd call essence a naïve concept,
and laud the freeing nature of social construction,
but I'm not convinced that that's all there is,
as I watch you not tip the waiter, stepping in front
of someone to make a point about ancient Greece.

Awake in a Strange Landscape

Deep in my gut,
large stones scrape each other
to dust at night, rising into coughs
until my mouth is white chalk in the morning.

    Something has become intolerable.

I work as a waitress.
Every day, rich customers,
their fingers beckoning me like feathers.

    The dishwasher empties trash in the back.

I work with people too young to remember
Vietnam, or even Watergate.
They speak in airy voices of becoming
accountants, going into advertising.
They say it must have been neat
to live in the sixties.

    The black cooks rap to L. L. Cool J in the kitchen.

The fat woman wants to order half of a grilled sandwich.
I tell her we will have to throw the other half away.
She says that's okay, waving her diamond hands,
her Talbot's bag at her side.

    I am heaping trash on the dishwasher.
    He is still singing under piles of remains,
    wet cigarettes soaked with coffee,
    everything that is used.
    With strong black arms, he scrapes the blood-
    colored lipstick from wine glasses
    for three dollars an hour.

The waitresses are talking about how fat they are,
about working out, about spring break,
about the real job they will get.

> I don't know how to tell them what I'm thinking.
> I'm thinking of the taste of chalk in the morning,
> I'm thinking that we are Americans,
> lost steer crashing into landscape,
> herds rumbling to some black sea.

AN ABORTION ATTEMPT BY MY MOTHER

Rolling side to side in my warm mother,
the juices of life pulsing through my veined skin,
wild juices of calves' tongues and loose
stretchy kid skin like young gray wrens.
I drink unborn water in the Garfield back room
in the dark while my mother cries.

The prodding of wolves' teeth,
eyes red and ailing, the shaking
of orange clay and cracked slate, the loosening,
exposing the underground creatures to full sky,
the greased worms are screaming, the dead moles stay dead.
This is the feeling.

MORNING RADIO

It is morning again
and the child wakes to a light
that prickles her spine,
doesn't bathe it in warmth
like it's supposed to.
There's a poetry show on the radio.
Her mother leaves for work,
and the familiar sounds begin;
the slow turn of her doorknob
like a liquid switch inside her,
the slap of her father's slippers
on the tile floor, the sound of her own breath
as she squeezes her eyes shut and prays to disappear,
then the ever slightest swish of air
as the belt of her father's robe passes
her face, the last thing she hears
before he gets on top of her.
Someone's reading a love poem on the radio.
Today the FCC is protecting this child
from the bad words, the words she hears
in school, bringing her pleasant poems
to be raped by, and the radio stations comply.
As she squints her eyes shut,
she is no closer to naming
this thing that happens to her,
she is the only child in this room,
the only child in the world.

FIFTEEN

the first time is so scary
with your legs up in the air
no one ever told you what
a speculum was and back then
you had to take everything off
no one told you then
not to go to a man   besides
your sister said this
was a good doctor

so when he was down there staring
at you and telling you   you were prettier
than your sister you thought
it was strange but not wrong
and when he played with your nipples
and talked about breast feeding
even though you weren't pregnant
you listened to him

and when he asked you
what you and your boyfriend did   exactly
you thought he needed to know
but when he shoved his tongue
down your throat   you knew
that you had stepped into a hole so dark
like being cold when it's not cold
like when your skin wants to go
inside your body
like never saying a word
for years

FERRY AT NIGHT

Water sounds, the bow splits the water;
the flapping of flags, a wet gunshot.
Don't wait. Go into the dark water.
Wash yourself with the sand
of water, the wash of black. Don't think
of reason, don't think of danger.
Find the black swallows that fly
the black ocean. Hear the flapping,
flapping thick with water, armies of swallows
moving in schools, rocking the water,
next to the dark fish,
next to the thickened rope.
Under the crests are the bones
of the dead, floating and rocking,
slime of wet bone,
seduction of wet skin.
Return to the sense of moon and fish,
wash yourself in a hundred rolling dark hands,
rolling and waving, the dark hands
of a mother—your hands,
yours.

WATCHING MY FATHER

I watch him look out the picture window,
hands in his pockets, he is staring out.
I think maybe he's admiring the pear tree
that has lasted another summer of tentworms,
the hours of burning nests, white webs crackling.

He watches the tall pines that he planted as seedlings,
and thinks of the darkness, the end of this sight.
He says things like, *I feel it slipping away*
and I listen. He said once, *There is only one way
this can end, Jan.* I began to protest,
then turned my head to rest.

Twice a week we go to radiation therapy.
He brings candy to the nurses, praises their patience.
The one is a dancer, he asks about her shows.
They call his name, he walks through the door.

I save him in my waking dreams on those days.
Like a child, I wish for angels,
soft beds of sweet flowers, the end of all pain.
I dream an angel's hand, a breath of fiber,
whatever could make him whole: a day without work,
a chance to relive the years that strangled him quiet.

The therapy doors shut. I delude myself.
This is the summer his chest is burning.
Technicians scorch him, aiming their machines
at the webs in his chest, the spot near his heart
where his lungs breathed the steel mills,
where he keeps whatever it is he clutches at,
the unexpressed, dirty air.

FOG

What I yearn for is suspension.
I want to be fog,
a loose glove that holds the wetness,
that hangs from nothing in the grey
morning sky, a low secret
in the valley;
particles so close together, air so thick
that the senses cease. I wish for a second
to lose the steadiness of my breath,
happy to see grey and nothing else—
nothing but the thick grey gel of fog.

Fog surrounds me like a lover's hand
over my face as limbs grab and slash
in passion, reaching out for any softness,
and hardness, for stray hair, sheets between legs,
all the while lost again in the beautiful fog.
When I die, I think I will move
through this same fog.
My eyes will be fog grey, my speech will steam
out in the twelve languages of the uncertain.

Dream with No Words

So we were in this pizza parlor,
Marlon Brando in these stone-washed brown leather jeans,
twenty years younger with no shirt, his belly hanging
one inch over his jeans at the point of perfect beauty.
Me, a teenager fumbling in the bathroom,
my black hair cut at a diagonal to the chin,
feeling ugly, but I wanted him.
I walked straight up to his chest hair,
he flung me on the dirty linoleum,
took me from behind, my face on the brown squares
of the pizza parlor floor, wishing and grunting,
wanting and rocking without speech,
no words, the relief of no words.

SUCKING

Sap is running out of the pine trees
like cum—and I know someone is coming right now,
screaming pleasure while I walk on this gravel path,
while insects stick in this golden sap of tree wound,
someone is sucking on someone's breast, someone's cock, lost
in the original comfort, lips urging and repeating
like every blue vein, while grey bark falls dead from trees
and everything fills with blood, the renegade stream
that cuts through the length of night
as we walk around alone
we suck the air
we suck on nothing.

Self-Hatred

overgrown, hairy birds
thump around, things with masks,
tracks in the dirt, one two three four,
painted designs overlap, overlap,
straight lines crossing other straight lines,
baskets full of dried pears hard as nickels.
I eat them. They scrape my mouth bloody.
I eat three more. I am an old Indian,
my headdress too heavy.
Owl feathers fly as I fall to the ground.
Birds peck at my bloody mouth.

WALKING IN SHADE

After he died, he was still
walking around.
There was a coarse blackness
where his eyes used to be.
All time was shaded. He yearned
for light and shadow, for the same
distinction that used to annoy him.
Often, he would touch himself,
his stomach warm and distended,
his genitals gone, melted
into a smoothness between his legs.
There was no speech here, no need
for food, only touching and hearing.

Walking around, the ground felt like sand.
Sometimes there was a wild flapping,
like the sound of heavy birds.
He could hear the feathers and sand,
feathers and sand, he didn't know how
to think about this place. He never believed
in things he couldn't see, like witches,
white magic, his wife's intuition.
Now his hands throb warm as he dreams
of his wife's brown hair, his hands
the center of desire, a liquid spot
in his palm pulsing during high winds,
or sometimes when the Others moan
their low moan, their soft mourning sound.
He misses his children. He wants to place
his palm on the face of another, he mourns
the waste of his life.

Wanting to Continue

Sometimes it seems to be this simple:
a peach in a clear glass bowl,
resting in the center of it,
the shades of orangish red, a glimpse
of yellow, the imprints of genetics,
the indentation from the quick grasp
of the worker's hand, the soft spot
of purple, the beautiful discoloration.

I lift the bowl and see even
the peach bottom, the point of contact,
and it is all right in front of me,
the glorious rub of peach fuzz, why we must
fall in love with ourselves and each other;
At once it becomes all relationships that ever existed,
the perfection of your hand petting my neck,
especially the stumble of your fingers,
the recovery to a smooth path, the tracing of shapes
that repeat themselves in patterns that
physics hasn't figured out—
the wanting to continue,
the wanting to please.

III

Be insatiable.
Then: Save yourself; others you cannot save.
—Adrienne Rich

SAVING THE CRIPPLED BOY

Tenth-grade field trip, I'm stuck
in the back of the chartered bus
with one-armed Bob Saunders, ten
rows away from the waves of my friends.
There I was, sharing the seat
with his hook of a hand,
his flesh-colored arm-like arm,
was it plastic, what was it made of,
we were sixteen, but it wasn't just
his arm—he was short, his hair
was greasy, he wouldn't talk to anyone.
And who would ever love him, had he ever
kissed a girl—would he ever kiss anyone?
Years before I knew about *mercy fucks,*
somewhere between New York City and Hampton,
it started, and we necked all the way home
from Springdale, the whole time, the bolts
in his arm clicked on the rim of the bus window,
Bob's tongue poking and pushing like
a hyperactive worm in my mouth, me afraid
his arm would flap over me like a hard dead person,
the whole time my good deed burying me, I wanted
to save him, just to save him, and now we were
both alone, covered with our benchwarmers,
Bob half on top of me in the cold vinyl seat,
I felt him get hard—small and hard, and
what had this become, I wanted blazing sanctimony,
saving the crippled boy with each plunge of

my normal tongue, but now I was saying, *Look,*
this is what you can't have, not for real,
this is for today, and I grew small and hard,
and thought of my boyfriend at home, my best
friend, Patty, and my sick, ailing heart.

WHAT I WANT

I want to drug all the tellers at Mellon Bank.
I want to tell the crazy guy at the Balcony,
the one who really was in prison for eight years in Turkey,
that it's okay to draw on his placemat.
I want him to have the whole restaurant to himself,
his head bent over his artwork, two inches
from ink drawings of streets and ships.
I want to tell my mother that I'll never buy a house
and that my heart is good.

I want to cover myself
with black petals
and lie still on cold dirt
and blend into ten languages,
and rest.

Introducing You to My Dead Father

—for Don

In the dream you were a spotted dog
with a curved lip that held a secret,
sort of like yours in real life.
My father was lying, bony and white
on a spare mattress in the next room
as I carried you to meet him.
He recognized you, but couldn't take the play
of a new puppy, the frisking and tumbling
as you fumbled all over him.
There were angels everywhere.

I picked you up and held you.
I remember now that you slept in my arms,
that I carried you to bed, arranged toys and pillows
around you, and told you to sleep *here*.
When you wake up, you will be facing this window,
you will be able to see forever.

Breaking the Skin

A woman stands near a large window,
staring out into an open space.
Today she is thinking about color,
she watches hills roll into each other,
wonders at these shades of green,
sweet rich green deepening to black.
She wants to taste green,
to drape herself in whatever green is.

If she would try to squeeze green into words, it would be:

> Green
> sitting straight in a high-backed chair
> teeth breaking the skin of an apple
> not lying about anything

> Black-green
> the underside of leaves
> waiting a long time to speak
> crawling through high grass in a dream

How can she explain where longing meets stillness?
Along the horizon a thin band of light
rims the hill and makes her want everything.
Who would she speak to of this?

AFTER SEX ON A TRAIN

canadian rockies fill
my window I am naked
eating blueberry muffins
sipping coke and smelling sperm
lakes and pines no birds fly past
I think of wild blueberries
bleeding juice through pale yellow
the yellow that's almost white
my calves bruised from holding on
rivers moving swollen white
rail ties lie in piles and I
sniff the musk that we all want
telephone poles bending toward
water the white birch the pines

LOVE POEM

Looking at you,
I feel the wind of a hundred birds taking off,
the large wingspread, the abandon at the moment
of liftoff, the air packed tight with wanting to fly.

Looking at you,
I think of a blues singer
holding her own hands as she sings,
her eyes closed with longing,
her red lips offering beauty to the world,
her black satin dress falling halfway off her shoulder.

Looking at you,
something separates inside me,
familiar voices crack
and fall into the valley of unwanted things.

I think now I can
wear my red dress again.
It's simple and cotton but
it always meant desire to me.
I'll wear red and some silver necklace
that's much too large. I'll eat a lot of pasta.
I'll dance much too long.

VISITING MY FATHER A FEW DAYS
BEFORE HIS OPERATION

I walk the cement steps to my father's house,
past the wall of stones around the garden,
red granite holding back the packed earth.
I remember a softer time,
when he and the neighbor next door
were building that wall, hauling
rock, my father standing with his foot against a spade,
pounding down beer after beer,
his chest shiny with sweat, an old rag hanging
from his back pocket and always a hat
that said "Budweiser" or "Shit-Kicker."
He would smile an easy smile and say,
What do you think, Jannie?
and I would always say, *Looks good,*
and admire it with him.

Now I'm walking past that wall, past
the flowering pear tree, past the flowering
crabapple, the ones my father planted just for blossoms.
He said the birds could eat the marble fruit.
I'm walking into the simple ranch house
where my parents have lived for thirty years.
My father has just turned seventy, now he sits
arms folded over belly, coughing and cursing
his coughs. He just doesn't feel right,
he says. In a few days they will operate,
lift his arms from his chest, and cut into his lung.

He jumps up, he has something to give me,
he says. I think of a will, safety-deposit box keys,
but he hands me three boxes. I open to the bright cloth

of his World War II medals. I try to see him,
a thin man in navy fatigues, fighting
in the Asian Pacific Theater Campaign,
this white-haired man in a blue cardigan,
bounding from troop carrier to beaches, embracing his rifle.
One medal says, "Freedom From Fear And Want" on the back,
and I wish it for my father.

GHOST ORCHID

If I could float with ghost
Orchids in Florida,
Hang lush from the custard-
Apple trees, waxy and
Leafless and breathing chalk,
I would sway through black nights,
Arching toward earth from the
Weight of my buds, I would
Hang, a snow white death frog
In this sleeping forest.
I would leave my branches
To fly with the night hawks,
Just a flea, I would suck
Sticky wild blood of hawk.
Then I'd return, full and
Spindling toward you, fragile
And green as my yellow
Stamen scents the night air.

THE SPACE THAT REMAINS

I'm looking for a machine to change my life.
My friend, John, tells me
that his computer saves so much time,
that he can barely write without it now—
the automatic spell-check, the punctuation check,
the new ease of editing with recall and delete,
the holy convenience—but John, I say, what happens
if you're using a paper and pen, you want to look
up a word but you can't find the dictionary, so
you walk around, past a box of old papers, you find
a letter from a friend who has died, you start to feel
something, you walk back to the page, you continue
your poem in a way that could never have happened
if you'd stayed in your chair? John is shaking his head,
I want to tell him I'm not afraid of change, just in love
with some kind of wandering. I think of my friend, Yvonne,
a woman I work with, who asked me what
to buy her boyfriend for Christmas this year.
What about a velour cover for his car phone, I said.
I'm glad Doug has a car phone, she said, *His car
broke down last week, and we were able to call for help,
right from the car*—Yes, but what if you left the car,
went for a walk, had great sex in a ditch down the road,
rediscovered a particular part of the universe that night?
As Yvonne huffed, I dreamed of running to the slow places,
or just walking to the window to see what was there.

A Waitress' Instructions on Tipping or
Get the Cash Up and Don't Waste My Time

Twenty percent minimum as long as the waitress doesn't inflict bodily harm.

If you're two people at a four top, tip extra.

If you sit a long time, pay rent.

Double tips for special orders.

Always tip extra when using coupons.

Better yet, don't use coupons.

Never leave change instead of bills, no pennies.

Never hide a tip for fun.

Overtip, then tip some more.

Remember, I am somebody's mother or daughter.

No separate piles of change for large parties.

If people in your party don't show up, tip *for* them.

Don't wait around for gratitude.

Take a risk. Don't adjust your tip so your credit card total is even.

Don't ever, ever pull out a tipping guide in public.

If you leave 10% or less, eat at home.

If I call a taxi for you, tip me.

If I hang up your coat for you, tip me.

If I get cigarettes for you, tip me.

Better yet, do it yourself.

Don't fold a bill and hand it to me like you're a big shot.

Don't say, *There's a big tip in it for you if . . .*

Don't say, *I want to make sure you get this,* like a busboy would steal it.

Don't say, *Here, honey, this is for you*—ever.

If you buy a $50 bottle of wine, pull out a ten.

If I serve you one cocktail, don't hand me 35¢.

If you're just having coffee, leave a five.

T-shirts

I keep my father's T-shirts
in a brown paper bag in the hall,
in between the bathroom and the bedroom.
There is no place for them since he has died.
They are big, extra large, almost full of him,
with his uneven beer belly and his mottled skin.
One says, "The Best Beer Drinkers Are From Whitehall."
I used to buy these shirts for my Dad,
along with a bottle of Imperial or some imported beer.
He always said, *Why do you waste your money on this foreign stuff?*
After three they all taste the same.
Another shirt is speckled with paint and says,
"I Can't Be Fired—Slaves Must Be Sold."

They seem to smell like him, a smell I carry with me now.
I couldn't give them to the Salvation Army with the eight bags
of his suits and shoes, his blue-and-white-striped bermuda shorts
and his gum shoes that I always thought looked silly.
So I leave them in the hall. I greet them
as I walk into my apartment, maybe with just a glance,
or maybe I stare for a few seconds.
Sometimes at night when I can't sleep,
I go to the bag and sort through them,
hold them to my face
and say hello.

STANDING BY THE MCKENZIE RIVER AT NIGHT

Even at night you can see the foam.
A white gleam floating all on its own,
the wild rushing of water over rocks;
the thick whiteness changes shape
from twisting Chinese dancers—
deep white flowers moving and breathing—
to a table full of stiff men in robes.
I think of the Last Supper and feel stupid.
I think I see my father at home
hovering above his body.
I want to still the whiteness and
I want it to roar.

BLUE DRESS

Blue dress, white
laced V crossing
my bodice, I loved
that dress. Selfish,
my mother said. Wrong
to care so much for
a dress. I didn't say
the color soothed
my questions. Deep blue,
fresh cotton on
my skin, blue pleasure
rubbing the dress
between my legs
folds into folds
after church
in my bedroom.
Blue dress.

Not Thinking About Gardenias

I am not in the mood
to think about gardenias today,
to even consider the flow of the word,
with its wide-open vowels.
I don't want to talk about it,
the glossy leaves that always look wet,
the white flowers that drink the tears
of angels to grow bold and soft;
I would rather hide in the strangeness
of wood: the twists of the grain, the visions
of dead hogs and seedy brown volcanoes,
the lines that make no sense,
the beautiful abandonment.

ASKING THE DEAD FOR HELP

The horses are standing still now,
droop-backed and silent in silver stalls.
I think they are dead, not asleep.
I think they are mourning the world,
their manes hanging sadly on their necks
like someone else's unwashed hair.
Here in this pine-filled valley
there is no relief from the still-life.
I see myself, other humans standing
motionless in their stalls, silent in the big valley,
breathing the grand dust, now and then
sucking the air for something new.

I visit my father's grave and stare at the aging spruce,
wondering what it is we say when there's nothing to lose.
I want to hear the final breath of the living,
all of a man's life condensed to a sigh,
the words uttered at the moment between worlds,
the only words that can save us.

THE FLOWER GARDEN

This pattern has become hers:
three steps from the bricks to the clover field,
and then the world becomes only her
and the names of the things she loves.
Violets, then rose of sharon, pink impatiens
on the right, and later on, wild ferns
clustered awkwardly as if out of place.
This place is a gift that must not be questioned.
The slight breeze carries the scent of honeyed wood,
at least that's what she has named it.
She walks through the thick air,
thinking of the joy of not breathing during sex,
the heaviness of pollen. She wonders how many others
have these gardens. At the end, a vine-dressed wall,
the shine of leaves.

ONE HAND ON THE DOOR

If you climb over the edge of the dune,
you will come to a slope that will comfort you.
It may remind you of the curve of your lover's lip,
long passed into tightness.

Or maybe the predictable roundness
of your mother's hand as she led you through
your early world, the hand that said, *Take pleasure
in the curves, sink in, if you can.*

Now you're afraid of the black and white of it,
the play of sun and shadow on colorless days;
Because your mother's hand never really said that,
and the familiarity of absence is just not enough anymore.

On good days, you pray for right combinations,
on bad ones, you retell the stories that cripple you;
With one hand on the door, you dream of openings,
with the other, you carry small offerings:
your life thus far.

FREE WORLD

When restraints fall away like holy days,
and my self, a cluster of clutched petals,
presses in, peels away, and layers thickly
an unforgiving floor—I shudder
for those few green moments of self
on the way to clustering of a different name.
What is inside this severe wanting,
this wanting to re-remember touch,
when transgression slides its ravenous blue
tongue into normal skin and you
peel my expected blouse from me,
and see the someone you've never seen,
the hardened bud of whoever I thought I was,
as we hit against our pitted skin in the dark
and call it love—whatever lets us breathe
this dark together—what is this soft touch,
after years of trying on, taking off, wishing
to go back? Whose forbidden is this,
that falls to the open floor, like a shade
settling on a bedroom wall, as we rub ourselves
into the calm of death, free world, pale niche
of surrender.

ACKNOWLEDGMENTS

The author and publisher wish to acknowledge the following publications in which some of these poems first appeared: *5 AM* ("after sex on a train," "Fifteen Minutes at the Dairy Mart"); *The Louisville Review* ("Mad River"); *National Poetry Competition* ("Self-Hatred"); *Nimrod* ("Fog," "Love Poem," "Not Thinking About Gardenias," "Visiting My Father a Few Days Before His Operation," "What We Can Count On"); *Pendulum* ("Blue Dress," "Breaking the Skin," "fifteen," "Pittsburgh Poem," "T-shirts"); *Pittsburgh Post-Gazette* ("A Waitress' Instructions on Tipping or Get the Cash Up and Don't Waste My Time," "The Space That Remains"); *Pittsburgh Quarterly* ("An Abortion Attempt by my Mother," "As If That's All There Is," "What I Want"); *Poetry East* ("Introducing You to My Dead Father"); *Seattle Review* ("Awake in a Strange Landscape," "Morning Radio"); and *Southern Poetry Review* ("Ghost Orchid," "Ravenous Blue").

ANTHOLOGIES

The Denny Poems 1993–1994 ("If This Is Sex, It Must Be Tuesday"); *For a Living: Poetry of Work* ("A Waitress' Instructions on Tipping or Get the Cash Up and Don't Waste My Time"); and *A Gathering of Poets* ("Asking the Dead for Help").

I would like to express my appreciation to the Pennsylvania Council on the Arts; the Arts and Humanities Council of Tulsa, Oklahoma; and Ucross Foundation, Clearmont, Wyoming, for fellowships and support which helped me to write these poems. I would also like to thank Maggie Anderson, Patricia Dobler, Lynn Emanuel, Nancy Koerbel, Ed Ochester, Deb Pursifull, and Judith Vollmer for helpful comments on these poems; special thanks to Sharon Doubiago, Barry Lopez, W. D. Snodgrass, and Gary Snyder for their support; my parents, Mildred and Robert T. Beatty; Paul Baxter, Joe Browne, Joe DiFiore, and David Goldstein for extraordinary support; Bob Feldman, Muzz Meyers and the staff of the Shadyside Balcony; Don Rosenzweig for his generous help with graphics and design; Michel Tsouris for her wonderful paintings; the In-a-Different-Voice Girls; Kathy Staresinic and Paul Baumgartner; Madison Brooks for her courage; Carole Coffee for her wandering spirit; Rhoda Mills Sommer for showing me the way; and Don Hollowood, the love of my life.

JAN BEATTY ———————————

       has held jobs as a welfare caseworker, a rape counselor, and a nurse's aide. She has worked in maxium security prisons, hoagie huts, burger joints, jazz clubs, and diners. She won the 1990 Pablo Neruda Prize for Poetry and two fellowships from the Pennsylvania Council on the Arts. Her chapbook, *Ravenous*, won the State Street Press chapbook prize for 1995.

PITT POETRY SERIES

Ed Ochester, General Editor

Claribel Alegría, *Flowers from the Volcano*
Claribel Alegría, *Woman of the River*
Debra Allbery, *Walking Distance*
Maggie Anderson, *Cold Comfort*
Maggie Anderson, *A Space Filled with Moving*
Dorothy Barresi, *The Post-Rapture Diner*
Jan Beatty, *Mad River*
Robin Becker, *Giacometti's Dog*
Siv Cedering, *Letters from the Floating World*
Lorna Dee Cervantes, *Emplumada*
Robert Coles, *A Festering Sweetness: Poems of
     American People*
Billy Collins, *The Art of Drowning*
Nancy Vieira Couto, *The Face in the Water*
Jim Daniels, *M-80*
Kate Daniels, *The Niobe Poems*
Kate Daniels, *The White Wave*
Toi Derricotte, *Captivity*
Sharon Doubiago, *South America Mi Hija*
Stuart Dybek, *Brass Knuckles*
Odysseus Elytis, *The Axion Esti*
Jane Flanders, *Timepiece*
Forrest Gander, *Lynchburg*
Richard Garcia, *The Flying Garcias*
Suzanne Gardinier, *The New World*
Gary Gildner, *Blue Like the Heavens: New & Selected Poems*
Elton Glaser, *Color Photographs of the Ruins*
Hunt Hawkins, *The Domestic Life*
Lawrence Joseph, *Curriculum Vitae*
Lawrence Joseph, *Shouting at No One*
Julia Kasdorf, *Sleeping Preacher*
Etheridge Knight, *The Essential Etheridge Knight*
Bill Knott, *Poems, 1963–1988*
Ted Kooser, *One World at a Time*
Ted Kooser, *Sure Signs: New and Selected Poems*
Ted Kooser, *Weather Central*
Larry Levis, *The Widening Spell of the Leaves*
Larry Levis, *Winter Stars*
Larry Levis, *Wrecking Crew*
Walter McDonald, *Counting Survivors*
Irene McKinney, *Six O'Clock Mine Report*
Archibald MacLeish, *The Great American Fourth
     of July Parade*

Peter Meinke, *Liquid Paper: New and Selected Poems*
Peter Meinke, *Night Watch on the Chesapeake*
Carol Muske, *Applause*
Carol Muske, *Wyndmere*
Leonard Nathan, *Carrying On: New & Selected Poems*
Kathleen Norris, *Little Girls in Church*
Ed Ochester and Peter Oresick, *The Pittsburgh Book of
       Contemporary American Poetry*
Sharon Olds, *Satan Says*
Gregory Orr, *City of Salt*
Alicia Suskin Ostriker, *Green Age*
Alicia Suskin Ostriker, *The Imaginary Lover*
Greg Pape, *Black Branches*
Greg Pape, *Storm Pattern*
Kathleen Peirce, *Mercy*
David Rivard, *Torque*
Liz Rosenberg, *Children of Paradise*
Liz Rosenberg, *The Fire Music*
Natasha Sajé, *Red Under the Skin*
Maxine Scates, *Toluca Street*
Ruth Schwartz, *Accordion Breathing and Dancing*
Robyn Selman, *Directions to My House*
Richard Shelton, *Selected Poems, 1969–1981*
Reginald Shepherd, *Some Are Drowning*
Betsy Sholl, *The Red Line*
Peggy Shumaker, *The Circle of Totems*
Peggy Shumaker, *Wings Moist from the Other World*
Jeffrey Skinner, *The Company of Heaven*
Cathy Song, *School Figures*
Leslie Ullman, *Dreams by No One's Daughter*
Constance Urdang, *Alternative Lives*
Constance Urdang, *Only the World*
Michael Van Walleghen, *Tall Birds Stalking*
Ronald Wallace, *People and Dog in the Sun*
Ronald Wallace, *Time's Fancy*
Belle Waring, *Refuge*
Michael S. Weaver, *My Father's Geography*
Michael S. Weaver, *Timber and Prayer: The Indian Pond Poems*
Robley Wilson, *Kingdoms of the Ordinary*
Robley Wilson, *A Pleasure Tree*
David Wojahn, *Glassworks*
David Wojahn, *Late Empire*
David Wojahn, *Mystery Train*
Paul Zimmer, *Family Reunion: Selected and New Poems*